Northern Ireland

Edited By Holly Sheppard

First published in Great Britain in 2019 by:

 Young**Writers**® Est. 1991

Young Writers
Remus House
Coltsfoot Drive
Peterborough
PE2 9BF
Telephone: 01733 890066
Website: www.youngwriters.co.uk

FOREWORD

Here at Young Writers, we love to let imaginations run wild and creativity go crazy. Our aim is to encourage young people to get their creative juices flowing and put pen to paper. Each competition is tailored to the relevant age group, hopefully giving each pupil the inspiration and incentive to create their own piece of creative writing, whether it's a poem or a short story. By allowing them to see their own work in print, we know their confidence and love for the written word will grow.

For our latest competition Poetry Wonderland, we invited primary school pupils to create wild and wonderful poems on any topic they liked – the only limits were the limits of their imagination! Using poetry as their magic wand, these young poets have conjured up worlds, creatures and situations that will amaze and astound or scare and startle! Using a variety of poetic forms of their own choosing, they have allowed us to get a glimpse into their vivid imaginations. We hope you enjoy wandering through the wonders of this book as much as we have.

CONTENTS

Scarlett Rose Ronaldson (10) 61
Tom Patterson (10) 62
Heidi Pollock (10) 63
Grace Young (10) 64

Newbuildings Primary School, Newbuildings

Chloe Louise Neely (10) 65
Cerys Hamilton (10) 66
Lauren Caroline Browne (10) 68

St Brigid's Primary School, Cloughmills

Rory Blaney (10) 69
Dara Waide (10) 70
Jack Hardy McAuley (10) 71
Clare McNeilly (10) 72
Conor McCann 73
Daniel Redmond (10) 74
Niamh Corr (11) 75
Erin Brennan (10) 76

St Mary's Primary School, Pomeroy

Eunan Beggs (10) 77
Chloe Murphy (10) 78
Daniel Cullen (10) 80
Caitlin Mary Stewart (10) 81
Olivier Koprowski (10) 82
Odhran Barrett (10) 83
Clodagh Carey (10) 84
Kirsty Scott (10) 85
Darragh Rafferty (10) 86
Caitlin Graham (10) 87
Oliver Thomas Grimes (10) 88
Aidan Devlin (9) 89
Ella-Mae Woods (9) 90

St Patrick's Primary School, Mullanaskea

Dara Flynn (10) 91
Jude Noel Patrick Trainor (9) 92
Lorcan Doherty (9) 94
Enya Moss (9) 96
Luke McCaffrey (10) 98
Shaun Fitzpatrick (10) 100
Broccan Leonard (9) 102
Emily O'Connor (11) 104
Leon Moore (8) 105
Isabella Wright (10) 106
Michael McGowan (9) 107
Adam Forster (9) 108
Grainne Gallagher (9) 109
Aisling Trainor (9) 110
Michael Cleary (11) 111
Tomás McGirr (9) 112
Oisín Murphy (9) 113
Ellie-Mae Clarkson (11) 114
Sophie Mae McGrory (10) 115
Charley Gilmurray (10) 116
Daniel Harvey (11) 118
Rian John McSorley (9) 119
Patrick Toal (9) 120
Makayla Lealan (10) 121
Kilian Trainor (8) 122
Cormac Cox (8) 123
Aoibhín Campbell (9) 124
Ryan McCann (11) 125
Hannah Hobbs (8) 126
Hannah Lynch (9) 127
Cathy Britton (10) 128
Ellen Cleary (9) 129
Robert Balfour (9) 130
Charlie Keegan (9) 131
Bella Maye Abraham (11) 132
Carágh Mary-Kate Sliman (9) 133
Alex Beacom (7) 134
Sorcha Leonard (8) 135
Russell Mikiewicz Lumayad (8) 136
Oran Fitzpatrick (10) 137
Daithí Shannon (10) 138

Niamh Murphy (10)	139
Ellie-Mae Murphy (11)	140
Cohen Murphy (10)	141
Tara Annie Mcmanus (8)	142
Eva-Alexandra Nelson (10)	143
Tara McCusker (9)	144
Eoghan Campbell (10)	145
Erun Farry (9)	146
Reuben Nathan Abraham (8)	147
Nathan Hanna (9)	148

Sunnylands Primary School, Carrickfergus

Freya Whitten (11)	149
Ellie McCrory (10)	150
Madison McClean (10)	152
Katie-Leigh Moore (10)	154
Katie Hill (11)	156
Josh Hildrew (11)	158
Jak Matthews (11)	160
Amelia Dougherty (8)	162
Erynne-Leigh McKeown (11)	163
Ellie Brown (10)	164
Jade Graham (9)	165
Yazmin Watson (9)	166
Paige Holmes (9)	167
Heidimarie Shaznay Hoey (11)	168
Anamika Ullas Nair (9)	169
Jorja Beck (8)	170
Jessica Ross (9)	171
Demi Sharkey (9)	172
Ollie McClean (9)	173
Kendra Allen (8)	174
Harry Speirs (9)	175
Kenzie Elliott (8)	176

THE POEMS

The Elephant And The Tea Party

I saw my friend, Elephant, the other day,
I was lost and he helped me find my way,
So I invited Elephant to my house for tea,
But it wasn't much fun, just him and me,
So I called my mum and called my stepdad,
And then I thought, *this isn't half bad*
We brought my sister because she is so sweet,
And Chloe enjoyed this lovely treat,
We had tea and cake and lots of fun,
Then we played games and Elephant won!
After a while my sister got sleepy,
And when that begins, she soon gets weepy
So Elephant hugged us all goodbye,
Then Chloe really started to cry,
"Don't worry," I said, "it's not the end.
Elephant will come back and he's bringing a friend!"

Abi King (10)

Abbey Primary School, Newtownards

A Teacher's Terror

It was a Monday morning,
When I stood and declared war on school,
So we advanced on the teacher,
And wrapped her up in wool.

Only her head was poking out,
She was so tightly tied,
And the little girl who liked her,
Cried and cried and cried.

We marched into the head's office,
Who trembled in a corner
"We'll go for Mrs Pats next," I hissed,
"whatever you do, don't warn her."

Some kids were running around the school
In red-hot rages,
Leaving behind them trails
Of broken pencils and ripped pages.

We ran into the playground,
Screaming our battle cry

Whoever stood before us
Would certainly die.

Some stew flew through the air,
Rebellious dinner ladies yelled, "Attack!"
But whatever happened,
We were going to fight back.

Some teachers had the common sense
To call the police,
And they arrived in their uniform,
Neat and proper and without a crease.

The police and pupils battled
All day and through the night
Rulers and forks flew through the air,
It really was a fright.

Finally, as the fight was coming to an end,
I heard a voice through the din,
"Come get your breakfast, darling,
For Monday morning is about to begin."

Hannah Joy Moore (10)
Abbey Primary School, Newtownards

The Hungry Aliens!

The aliens are in my back garden,
They come into my house,
They say that they are hungry,
So I look around the house
I give them what I find,
But it still is not enough
They go to the market
And eat all of their stuff
They come back home and wave goodbye
As they fly away in the sky
The next morning, we watch the news,
"The aliens are back, and that's breaking news!"

Nicky Robinson (11)

Abbey Primary School, Newtownards

My Party On Top Of The Mountain

My party on top of the mountain
Did not go as planned,
Crows stole my crisps,
The wind blew away my confetti
And the magpies drank my juice
As I thought nothing good could happen,
I realised that it was just a dream
And that it was a sign to not throw a party
On top of a mountain
So I found a better place to throw my party,
And it was the best party ever!

Holly Harrison (10)
Abbey Primary School, Newtownards

Purple Snow

You are probably wondering, purple snow?
That's a thing, you know,
First, I'll tell you how to make it,
You will need to bake and shake it,
You need frogs' eyes with a thick layer of salt,
If that makes you gag, it's not my fault
Next, you need a megalodon's tooth,
You might not believe me, but it's the truth
After that, a purple scale from a mermaid or
merman,
All mixed up in a glittering pan
Pick some lavender from a dark forest path,
After that, you might need a bath
The next ingredient is going to be tough,
You need the best snow from the top of Mount
Juff,
Haven't you heard of it? It's in Canada,
Mix it together and say tra-la-la,
If you don't want to make it, where do you go?
You can happily grab some from your local Tesco!

Charlotte Brisbane (10)
Anahilt Primary School, Hillsborough

The Land Of Dessert

I was dreaming one day about the Milkyshake
Way,
And a banana split boat,
In a milk chocolate moat,
Sailing past the toffee tower,
Twenty times an hour,
I was very very tired
But the food I desired
Wouldn't stop so that I could devour,
When the banana boat stopped
And I tried to take a bite,
Mum grabbed me by the arm
And gave me quite a fright
As I opened my eyes,
It was not night,
But Mum made it alright
With a chocolate delight.

Samara Wallace-Poole (10)
Anahilt Primary School, Hillsborough

Horses

H orses are beautiful animals
O nly some kick and bite
R iding is epic
S unset or sunlight
E veryone knows they are lovely
S ome snowy and white.

Katie Rutherford (10)

Anahilt Primary School, Hillsborough

Dave

My dog's called Dave,
And my name's Mave,
We're a crime-fighting team,
We know it's tough and we know it's rough.

So give us a shout,
We'll be there no doubt,
If someone breaks into your house,
And steals all your stuff, even the mouse.

Dave has mini bombs inside his paw,
And gets his meat extra raw,
He doesn't eat his broccoli,
He eats his vegetables sickly.

When we were sleeping through the night,
I woke up and heard a big, loud fright,
Through the night they stole Dave's tail,
So I went to hide up a bale,
After Dave had calmed down,
I came back with a big frown,
Sadly, Dave's tail was lost forever,
But I couldn't have told it any better.

Abigail Anderson (10)
Ballydown Primary School, Banbridge

My Tree Is A Superhero

My tree is a superhero,
His branches are massive, mighty muscles,
They are the size of tree trunks,
He is six-foot-four-inches tall,
His leaves are razor sharp ninja stars,
He has knuckle-dusters that shoot laser beams,
He has carbon fibre bark,
It makes him strong as steel,
His armour is the highest technology,
He has plasma guns coming from his shoulders.

The Terminator Robot Cat attacks him,
Supertree engages his force field
And he zapped the cat,
The cat ran away,
Then he went to his top-secret bunker
Deep under the sea,
To get his invisible jet,
And he saw the signal,
There must be trouble in the city,
It must be the deadly, mechanical dog
And his partners, the robot crows

They were robbing the bank!
Supertree grabbed the crows by their wings,
And he threw them like darts at the dog,
They exploded,
Supertree saved the day!

Sam Smyth (9)
Ballydown Primary School, Banbridge

The Red Velvet Muffin!

I live inside a chocolate cupcake,
Everything is delicious
I see sponge cake houses outside my house,
And my principal with a bright pink candyfloss afro
Walking his dog,
It's always cake for breakfast,
Cookies for lunch
And chocolate for dinner
There is never any dessert
Because healthy meals are unhealthy!
Everything here is happy,
Except for the Red Velvet Muffin!
He comes out every time there is a full moon,
He's got big, beady, revolting, red eyes!
The children get so scared
That they hide underneath their white chocolate beds!
But on this particular night,
I was feeling brave,
So I went outside and crept silently
Across the tasty, candy grass

And took a big bite out of him!
That was the end of him,
And my country was safe,
All thanks to me!
And let me tell you, he was very tasty!

Faith Anderson (10)
Ballydown Primary School, Banbridge

Opposite Land

Opposite Land, where the birds are seabound,
And the fish are flying around
Whales jumping and crashing to the ground,
Humans speaking like blah, blah, blah, to moo
Frogs going up, down and flying through,
Apples being grown already eaten
Bananas being found looking ancient,
Bikes going backwards causing accidents,
Trikes become motor trikes,
Cows taking flight,
Dictionaries having two pages with only 'at' and 'it'
Submarines flying,
Planes sinking,
Cats barking,
Sharks talking,
Babies drinking Coke,
While they hang up their coats
Cars driving upside down,
While sharks float around
Monkeys going to space,
Then running out of space

Crazy things are happening,
I think I'll join the monkey in space.

Lola Brown (10)
Ballydown Primary School, Banbridge

McDelicious In Space

I went into McDelicious in space
And this is what I saw,
A burger with sauces,
Whipped cream, beef, sausages,
Glue and googly eyes, oh yum!
With odours of garlic and troll breath,
How refreshing!

All of a sudden,
Came the most delicious chicken nuggets,
But I didn't see them for too long,
Because I ate them
They tasted like butter, rat teeth and so much
chicken,
Oh my, I can still taste it,
And then I saw the slimy, smelly, yummy chips,
Escaping with the vinegar,
So I ate them, along with the vinegar

I ate a mint alien and drank a cold, chocolate,
fizzy, wholesome slushie,
I also ate some spacemen

Why not?
I was about to go home
But the burger with googly eyes stole my ship,
So I had to take the bus.

Eoin Jeffers (10)

Ballydown Primary School, Banbridge

The Cyber Hamster!

Getting a pet hamster didn't go to plan.

I chose one with blood-red eyes,
Don't ask why,
He had the scent of diesel,
A glare of evil,
Coarse skin under a fluffy hide.

He was harmless,
Until I heard a deep, dark voice,
It was like a robotic squeak,
Yet a human voice.

It said, "Today the cage, tomorrow the food cupboard!"
Then I realised it was Cyan, my hamster!

I saw a bolt under his furry hide,
I screamed with fear and went to hide,
As petrifying, robotic eyes stared into mine,
His eyes hypnotising,
His face intimidating

He sent a booming hiss my way,
I fled and shut the door behind.

He's one hundred per cent evil,
To be continued.

Tilly Meade (9)
Ballydown Primary School, Banbridge

Fossil Island

Fossil Island is far away from home,
Very far if you ask me,
Everything is a fossil,
From the massive whales to the tiny mice,
They all move around eating and creeping,
The island is so dead and dry,
Everything is mouldy and bony
Even the food is dead,
You couldn't even live a week,
The water is so salty, as salty as can be
The centre of the island is a giant skull,
The centre is so dangerous,
Too dangerous for me
I know because I sat in a tree,
I got attacked by a polar bear,
A pteranodon and a rat,
There were piles and piles of gold,
I estimate a thousand,
But then I got eaten by a dragon,
So if I was alive, I'd sail back home and say,
Don't come to Fossil Island!

Lewis McCrum (10)
Ballydown Primary School, Banbridge

Dashing Doughnut

I was eating a doughnut yesterday,
When my doughnut suddenly sprang away!

And then my doughnut began to grow,
All the neon-like icing was dripping from the
dough!

And when my doughnut began to tumble,
The ground began to shake and rumble!

It dashed and it tumbled all around the park,
I ran after it because it was getting really dark!

And then I stopped and turned around,
And there was my doughnut, lying on the ground!

I picked it up and thought it looked scrummy,
I took a bite and mmm, it was yummy!

I felt the neon-like icing running down my throat,
I wonder what made my doughnut act the goat!

Martha Harper Simmance (10)
Ballydown Primary School, Banbridge

Demon Dog Mystery

I spotted a dog on Gumtree,
Is this what I see?
Could it be a demon dog,
Or is it just me?

Let's go see this dog today,
At least it's just five minutes away,
Oh, yes, we're there,
I hope it's not too scary,
Or else I'll lose my hair!

Yes, we're walking through the door,
I observed the dog leap off the floor
Next, I saw the owner come out,
It was significantly scary, I thought, to shiver and
shout!

I didn't enjoy this, I began to act,
This dog was dangerous, that was a fact.

One thing is for sure,
I'm not getting that dog

Oh no, the dog,
It's run away into the fog!

Alexandra Duffy (9)

Ballydown Primary School, Banbridge

Aliens

You think aliens live in space,
But I don't think it's true,
There might even be some in your smelly loo!

One day I saw a spaceship on the ground,
Inside, I found buttons and radars all around.

Do you dare to touch one?
If you do, the rocket might malfunction
And zoom off with you.

Have you thought about what aliens eat?
Well, their food is disgusting!
Like sticky toffee eyeballs
And ham and mould toasties.

Slimetember and Starummer are times for alien holidays,
When aliens come to Earth and party.

Next time you go to the loo,
Think of the intergalactic aliens looking up at you!

William Joseph White (9)
Ballydown Primary School, Banbridge

Right, Concentrate

"I'm the school boss, so listen,
Right, pupils, we have a big day ahead of us,
Right, concentrate,
Or I will stick you to the school gate,
First for the warm-up,
I want high knees
And twelve lunges to the kerb and back,
Now do ten press-ups,
And don't mess up!
Harder, Sienna! Harder!"
I'm so dehydrated,
I don't care,
"Now for the real thing,
You have to do ninety-nine laps,
Or you will get ninety-nine slaps!"
I'm so sweaty and frustrated,
"Now for stretching,"
I hate this part,
I think I might fart,
"Exercise over."
Finally!

Sienna Heasley (10)
Ballydown Primary School, Banbridge

Riding My Unicorn On A Cloud

I was riding my pony in my yard,
And then I accidentally fell off,
I landed on the ground and lay there asleep,
When I woke up on a cloud,
And my pony was a unicorn!
So I rode Willow on the cloud,
Even though it was quite risky
It got easy until I bumped into Lexie with Prisky,
So we rode our ponies together,
It was so much fun
We found a magic toad that we could not touch,
He told us he could help us get back home,
And we said yes, of course,
So we got down from the clouds
And told our mums what happened,
Of course, they didn't believe us!

Sarah Eakin (9)
Ballydown Primary School, Banbridge

The Bush Camper - A Fortnite Story

He wanted to land in Tilted Towers,
But there were gunshots every hour,
He found a chest and inside was a bush,
But there were two people trying to push
He tried to stay quiet while he plots,
But all he could hear were gunshots,
The storm was coming and the circle was shrinking,
He chugged his shield potions
And put on some suntan lotion
He felt really glad,
But I think one kill is bad,
Top two and of course, he needed the loo,
Ninja didn't stick the landing, 123 metres,
And that's how the Bush Camper got his first win.

Matthew Noah Toal (10)
Ballydown Primary School, Banbridge

The Day I Became A Cat

My mother kissed me good night,
But when I woke up, I had a big fright,
I had big, pointy cat ears,
But soon I had tears,
I jumped out of bed and scrambled downstairs,
Where my dish of fish was waiting for me,
The strange thing was, I enjoyed it
And gobbled it up
When mother was on the loo,
So I decided to do it too,
I drifted off to sleep beside the crackling fire,
I woke up with joy and happiness,
I was no longer a cat,
But then I became a dog
With a big bushy tail,
Whatever will I become next?

Sophia Ciara Sloan (9)
Ballydown Primary School, Banbridge

World Skating

I was skating on the moon, Saturn and Earth,
Ever since my mum gave birth
I started skating
Since I came out,
She began to shout
Ever since I began,
I never stopped.
Afterwards, I flew around Saturn's ring.
After then I flew to the moon,
From a crater to an alien's room...
Then there was a great big *boom!*
Suddenly I got shot
Onto a big jelly tot.
Then I bounced to something
Which was trying to bake,
Then I found out it was cake.
Yum! Yum!

Andrew McQuiston (9)
Ballydown Primary School, Banbridge

Super Three

Sam, Jack and James, known as the Super Three,
Were busy climbing sycamore trees,
When they heard the phone ring,
Ding, ding!
It was Mr Trump, moaning through the phone,
There had been a robbery at the bank,
So the Super Three grabbed their guns
And started to run,
Mr Drift robbed again,
Then all of a sudden,
Bang, Mr Drift was dead,
With two shots to the head
Once again, Super Three saved the day,
Hooray!

Thomas Mayne (9)
Ballydown Primary School, Banbridge

Outrageous Oscar On The Run

My dog, Oscar, is on the run,
Oh wow, this is gonna be fun!

I woke up this morning to a *woof*,
Oscar was growling at a bird on the roof

I ran downstairs to put on my shoes,
As I heard my mum say, "Oh, what did he do?"

Anyway, Oscar was on the run,
And he was trying to eat a chocolate bun!

Suddenly, I smelt a revolting poo,
Oh, and it's stuck to my dad's shoe!

Max Thomas Dobson (10)

Ballydown Primary School, Banbridge

Mushroom Land

One day I took a venture to Mushroom Land,
It looked pretty bland,
All I could see were mushrooms
All across the land,
I could see smoke coming from one,
It looked really thick,
But when I got closer,
It was all just a big trick!
There were cows all around me,
They said, "Who are you?"
Then they put me in a cage
Good thing I brought my teleporter,
Or I'd be a mushroom stew!

Jacob Gilham (10)
Ballydown Primary School, Banbridge

My Fast Food Turns Pink!

My fast food turns glistening,
Glittery, neon pink,
I took a wink and then a blink,
I then knew it was really true,
Now I don't know what to do!

I'll go home and take a rest,
I think that would be the best
So now I will settle down and try to process,
I'll get a friend so they can assess,
Twinkly glitter falling off me,
Eat pink fast food and you'll see!

Francesca Duffy (9)
Ballydown Primary School, Banbridge

Holiday On Mars

I was on Mars for a holiday,
It's all I could pay,
Floating away was an alien's craft,
I saw a mouse on top,
Don't be daft,
The aliens jumped out of the house
With the mouse
I showed them an egg,
He kicked it with his leg,
So I threw one up in the air,
And it landed in his hair
It went all over his head,
Then he dropped stone dead.

Aaron Robert Close (10)
Ballydown Primary School, Banbridge

New Year Christmas Cheer!

The fluttering robins with their fluffy fur,
Children taking their new teddies on a house tour,
Cosily cuddling on a cold winter's night,
With a bright red blanket being wrapped up tight

A crack and a creak as we all fall asleep,
I am tempted to take just a quick peep,
Hovering hooves stamp and stump,
And suddenly, I hear a great big thump

The delicate, beautiful snowflakes float up high,
And on the pan is a beautiful fry,
Big brown logs feeding the fire,
While kids sing sweetly in the choir

Fizzy drinks that make our tastebuds trickle,
Mum serves the gravy, "Oh, just a little."
Raising a toast to the new year,
We all cheer, "Happy New Year!"

Rebecca Culbertson (10)
Carrowreagh Primary School, Ballymoney

A Christmas Of Fun And Plenty!

Carrots for Rudolph and cookies for Santa,
Don't forget the milk, leave back the Fanta,
Hang up your stocking and put out the fire,
For the morning to come is our only desire
Dream sweet dreams of all your surprises,
As the sleeping starts, the magic sleigh arises!

The longest twenty-five days of your life are finally
over,
She got a doll and he got a toy Rover,
Delight in the dining of delicious Christmas dinner,
I can guarantee that it won't make you thinner,
Queen's speech quite unnecessarily loud,
See that snowy-looking cloud!

New snowmen delight in the yells of excited kids,
Pop! Goes the Shloer as they take off their lids,
Listen to the Christmas stories being told,
While bare trees shiver in the blistering cold

Bears have built their beds for slumber,
Already asleep in their caves of wonder.

Logs galore ready to feed the fire,
Pull your sledge up the hill, higher and higher
Numb fingers and red noses go trampling in,
To watch a Christmas movie with their kin
Cosy close to family in front of the crackling blaze,
Everyone's got the happy Christmas craze!

Unfortunately, the day must draw to a close,
And children are sent for their bedclothes
Dragging their heels, they get into their beds,
All the fun of the day fills their heads
As they close their eyes and give in to sleep,
The memories of the day they will cherish and
keep.

Yes! It's my birthday and guess what I got?
A pair of light-up gloves, believe it or not!
A scrumptious cake with eleven candles to blow,
Get ready, three, two, one, go!
A new year is now approaching fast,
And here come the fireworks, midnight at last!

Everyone knows school will return soon,
"Oh no!" back to the classroom of doom
New Year's resolutions that I don't think we'll keep,
The boredom of January's putting me to sleep
Although now our purses are half-empty,
This has been a Christmas of fun and plenty!

Sophie Shaw (11)
Carrowreagh Primary School, Ballymoney

A Happy Christmas

Children tiptoe up to their beds,
With the perfect present in their heads,
They run downstairs to look under the tree,
Boxes wrapped in patterns is all they see

Family members gather round,
Creating a buzz and a joyful sound,
It's the season we love this time every year,
Spreading the love and good cheer

Snowballs zooming through the big blue sky,
With spirits soaring sky high,
Frozen family fun on the slippery ice,
"Don't throw the snowball! Oi! That wasn't nice!"

Snowmen standing still and cold,
Some Christmas stories still untold,
We all come in for our Christmas tea,
"No thank you, sprouts are not for me!"

Daniel Callan (11)
Carrowreagh Primary School, Ballymoney

Frosty Winter

Open the window to a frosty chill,
Get ready to run, race down the snowy hill,
Children's faces delighted
And pray crunchy snow will stay,
Presents galore all over the floor,
What a perfect Christmas Day.

I see a lovely Christmas tree,
Families happy singing merrily,
Look outside, see lots of lovely snowflakes,
There are now lots of frozen lakes.

See an orange, flaming, blazing fire,
The snow is still rising higher and higher,
Lots of small, sneaky, small, squeaky mice,
Kids, take your parents' advice.

People seeing crystal-clear icicles,
Kids riding their new bicycles,
Lots of children going back to school,
Plenty of people saying school is not cool.

Lots of families having fun and cheer,
Kids hoping Santa will appear,
"Ho, ho, ho, here I come,
You kids have fun!"

Jacob McAuley (10)
Carrowreagh Primary School, Ballymoney

Magical Winter Day

Down on the ice,
There are snowball fights,
Then at the church and within,
Roof buried in snow,
Presents on show,
No one wants spring to begin!

Making new friends,
The fun never ends,
Darkness falls as the night draws near,
Kids go back for tea,
Screaming, "Leave some cake for me!"
Wishing St Nick will appear.

Opening the box
To find colourful socks,
And putting on the most colourful pair,
Dancing merrily around the house,
Even the cat's got a toy,
Eeek! A mouse,
Then go for a while to the Christmas fair.

Sarah-Jayne Madison (11)
Carrowreagh Primary School, Ballymoney

The Magical Misty Snow

Pitter-patter along the lane,
Through the deep, cold, powdery snow
The wintery fun is starting now,
My cheeks red with a wintery glow.

I look to the sky,
The white puffy snow is falling down
The ground is under the deep, cold snow,
I fell down and hurt my crown.

I went back home for my hot chocolate,
The marshmallows melting in the cup
Warming my hands and giving a blow,
Ready for me to drink it up.

On the ice, there is a snowball fight,
Trees wave in the wind overhead
Hands numb and tickly fingers,
Now it's time for my bed.

Kurt Martin (11)
Carrowreagh Primary School, Ballymoney

Nature's Winter

Hedgehogs hibernating as a prickly ball,
If you look at their home, how it is so small,
And bears are tucked up in their home,
All the animals are happily asleep in a safe zone

Puppies' paws are freezing,
And everyone is sneezing
We pitter-patter through the snow,
Hats and scarves are starting to blow

The countdown is on to New Year,
Flaming fireworks spreading good cheer,
As February zooms into spring,
And wasps are getting ready to sting.

Lee Alexander (11)
Carrowreagh Primary School, Ballymoney

Having Fun While We're Young

The beautiful snow is falling down,
Spreading fun all around,
Now it's time to have some fun,
Now it's time, while we're young.

Slippery slopes for skiing dreams,
While outside stands the snowy beams,
Time to climb the white-tipped mountains,
Or drink from the yummy chocolate fountains.

A crack and a creak as everyone goes to sleep,
As the sound of hooves patter on the roof,
Now it's time to have some fun while we're young.

Ben Callan (11)
Carrowreagh Primary School, Ballymoney

White Winter

Freezing flakes on the window pane,
A snowball fight erupts down the lane,
Snowballs flying everywhere,
They even get stuck in my hair.

Huge snowmen start to appear,
Everyone gives a joyful cheer,
A glorious dinner is on my plate,
I am even allowed to stay up late.

Unboxing presents from my friends,
I hope this fun never ends,
As jolly January is drawing near,
Christmas is nearly over, I fear.

Gemma McLaughlin (10)
Carrowreagh Primary School, Ballymoney

Winter

Skiing down the mountain,
Look how fast we go,
I am so happy playing in the snow,
Mum says we have to come inside,
But Riley and I try and hide,
Feeling bashful and free
As we ski around the willow tree,
I feel so great playing with my skates,
But marvellous, magnificent marshmallows
In hot chocolate awaits
Looking up into the sky so dark,
As the fireworks finish and the dogs bark.

Cameron Gregory (11)
Carrowreagh Primary School, Ballymoney

A Magical Winter

The winter is back, here we go,
The ground is covered in sparkling snow,
My numb fingers gathering the powdery white,
Crashing into the window, giving my mother a
fright.

I grab my sleigh, going up the hill,
When I get home, I feel pretty ill,
A cup of hot chocolate to keep me warm,
I'm in my house, waiting for the storm.

Thomas Sloan (11)
Carrowreagh Primary School, Ballymoney

Poem For The High Tackles

R ough as you can get
U nder the lights
G rass all over
B etter be at the shower after
Y ou will be sore after

H eight is a problem
I have never done it
G ood game after
H earts are needed

T ackles are important
A lways keep an eye out
C ards come out
K icking is important
L ong way from the posts
E ating is important before the game.

Jordan McGarvey (11)
Churchtown Primary School, Cookstown

The Snow Dog

The snow dog was at home
And it started snowing,
Then it was white,
And it disappeared from home,
Mum went out and said, "Where are you?"
The dog was back in five minutes
And that was that for a while,
Then a few days later,
Snow started to fall again,
Then the dog was covered in snow once more
And it did not disappear.

Alfie McFarland (11)
Churchtown Primary School, Cookstown

My Sheep

Standing in a field,
Feeding the sheep,
Munch, munch, yum, yum,
Counting sheep, one, two, three,
Oh no, one is missing,
Look high and low,
In ditches, rivers and sheds,
See a fluffy woolly ball,
Flying past the stars,
Zooming over the moon,
And landing back home.

William Wensley (8)
Churchtown Primary School, Cookstown

Snow, All Day Long

S lush, I don't like
N othing like snow
O ught to play with it
W ater, it turns into

Snow, most of us like, but not all of us,
It is fun to play with all day long,
Cold all day long but it is worth it,
Do you like snow?

Timothy Crawford (11)
Churchtown Primary School, Cookstown

Hatter's Hat

In, out, in out,
The needle goes as you sew,
Tick-tock, tick-tock!
The clock goes,
Who am I for? Who knows?
Tie a bow around my neck,
I'm done!
Back, forth, back, forth,
You take me every day,
I can't wait for another party.

Jodie Brown (11)
Churchtown Primary School, Cookstown

The Giant Talking Pizza

Walking down the street,
Not expecting who I would meet,
A giant, talking pizza coming my way,
He can walk and he can also play by the way,
He looked like a yummy pizza,
But the funny thing was,
He thought *I* was food,
And then I realised, oh no,
I was about to be a pizza's dinner for the day,
He made a dash for me,
But I was as quick as a flash,
Running into a shop,
Was my only hope,
Grabbing a cutter,
This would make the pizza stutter!
Oh, it really was a sharp cutter!
The pizza was super scared,
He just wanted to go back to his bed!
The pizza ran away,
Hoping I wouldn't see him any other day!

Jack Wasson (10)
Edwards Primary School, Castlederg

Pony Show In The Sky

Ding, ding! Zara Smyth on Jack,
I entered the arena to a thunderclap,
Wind in my ears, sun on my back,
Jack slowed down, I gave him a slap,
First jump, a big fluffy cloud,
Cleared it well,
My nerves calmed down,
Number two, a water jump,
Too much rain has made it a flood,
Jack reared to the left,
We missed the jump,
Went racing off over the rainbow hump,
Galloped around the Milky Way,
"Woah there, Jack,"
Was all I could say,
Jupiter, Venus, Mars passed by,
Cleared the stars, I thought I could fly,
But hit the moon with a great big thump,
Landed back on Earth with a bump.

Zara Elise Allen Smyth (9)
Edwards Primary School, Castlederg

The Bunny Is Hopping!

I woke up today,
Feeling quite sick,
I'm in a small cottage,
The walls extremely thick,
Wondered what had happened,
Why I was so sick?
I ran out the door,
Sprinting with fear,
Ran around the corner
And oh my dear!
I saw a giant bunny hopping,
Right for me,
Better run fast
Or I'd be eaten for tea,
He caught up with me,
His fur extremely soft,
I realised he had given me a hug,
Lovely as can be,
I thought he was a monster
That was about to eat me,
I looked left and right

I was in my room,
It was all a dream,
But secretly, I hoped he'd come back soon.

Leah Catherine Joan Magee (10)
Edwards Primary School, Castlederg

A Monster Party

It was a dark and stormy night
I tiptoed into the mansion
I clearly heard the sound of horses' hooves outside
I heard a loud noise like music
I entered the room the music was coming from
A group of skeletons were dancing gleefully
Frankenstein's monster was slowly putting his bolts back in
Dracula was happily drinking red juice...
Or I hope it was!
A werewolf was angrily chasing its own tail
A mummy was annoyingly making a rustling noise
A witch was cackling and she made a spell
A fishman quickly jumped in the pool
I left confused
I hope I never see a monster again,
Until next Halloween!

Logan McSorley (10)
Edwards Primary School, Castlederg

The Burger Fox And The Sauce Mouse

Quickly, a burger was made in a café,
It was a fox burger which had really tangy cheese,
Stringy lettuce,
Two beefy burgers,
Carefully, a box of sauce was carried in,
Slowly, the box was unloaded,
Out of the box appeared
A silly, little, magical sauce mouse,
Happily, it wandered across the counter,
The people in the magical café
Were loudly eating cow burgers,
Which were magical,
Quietly, the burger and the sauce
Jumped off the counter
And out into the magical world.

Joanne Rogers (10)
Edwards Primary School, Castlederg

Riding On A Shooting Star

Flying in the twinkling sky,
The galaxy amazingly black and high,
Looking at the shooting star,
Now I want to go quite afar,
When I know what is up above,
I suddenly fall in love,
My eyes briefly seeing the sun,
But now it's time for some fun,
Looking back at the trail,
Of the shooting star's tail,
Swiftly, the night sky moves,
I like to dance with the grooves,
I found Mars and Venus too,
Hope I didn't lose a shoe,
On Mars, I nearly died,
No aliens... They lied!

Lily Monteith (10)
Edwards Primary School, Castlederg

Pixie Trouble

Today I woke up early
Because I heard a thud,
A bright light came flying down my chimney,
I screamed, "Argh! It's a bug!"
Then I looked closer to find it was a pixie,
She was looking at me angrily,
And well, that was rude!
She started emptying my drawers,
Then she ripped up my books,
She threw all my shoes
And all my clothes out of the window,
Laughing mischievously,
She disappeared from view,
I hope I never see a pixie again.

Scarlett Rose Ronaldson (10)
Edwards Primary School, Castlederg

Imaginary Land

I woke up hungrily,
A breakfast appeared,
I thought of a fast car,
It appeared in front of me,
I thought of a friendly dinosaur,
It appeared, but it was not friendly,
I hopped into the car,
And put my foot on the pedal,
Then drove away,
But the dinosaur did not give up,
He followed me,
Then I remembered I can imagine anything,
I imagined it would get hit by a big meteor,
But it was a meatball!
Happily, it did the trick.

Tom Patterson (10)
Edwards Primary School, Castlederg

Underwater BBQ

The underwater BBQ did not go to plan,
I lit the BBQ and it went out,
The shark ate all the burgers,
The red sauce sank,
The fish ate all the sausage rolls,
The starfish ate the chicken nuggets,
I could not drink with my snorkel,
I couldn't eat the bread because it got all soggy,
It was a disaster!

Heidi Pollock (10)

Edwards Primary School, Castlederg

Shrink To The Size Of An Ant

An old lady gave me a bottle,
I don't know what it is,
I was worrying that night,
I took a little sip,
Is it me or is my room getting bigger?
I was so small,
I was smaller than an ant,
I don't know what to do,
It must be about that old lady.

Grace Young (10)
Edwards Primary School, Castlederg

Springtime

I love the smell of spring,
And listening to the birds sing,
The sunlight through the trees,
Makes me feel happy and bright,
I love the smell of spring,
And how the fresh cut grass smells,
The flowers come up
To say hello,
And grow into wonderful colours,
Colours of the rainbow,
Shine through the sunlight when it rains,
I love the weather in spring,
For it makes birds sing,
And flowers bloom,
For me to hear and for me to see,
This makes me feel happy and wonderful inside.

Chloe Louise Neely (10)
Newbuildings Primary School, Newbuildings

A Wee Funny Troll

There's a wee funny troll at the bottom of my
garden
I approached him cautiously,
He screeched, "I beg your pardon!
I'm only out playing, I'm really not staying," he said
As he scurried away on a beautiful sunny day.

He looks quite strange but he seems really cool.
I think he enjoys a swim in my lovely big pool
He wanders around the flowers,
I could watch him for hours
He doesn't seem to talk,
But lives under a rock

I would like to get to know him,
But he seems a bit dim,
When I get too close,
He disappears in a whim
His wee short legs and ginger curly hair,
Sprinting across the lawn, acting really rare

Hopefully one day, he'll like to be my friend,
And I can spend time with him until days end

I'm just a bit curious as to why he's out my back,
Maybe he is just lying low and enjoying all the
craic!

Cerys Hamilton (10)

Newbuildings Primary School, Newbuildings

The Sleepy Teacher

The teacher was in her classroom,
Her pupils were hard at work
Laying her head upon her hands,
She quietly fell asleep

Some of the pupils stopped their work,
To draw upon her face
Then they sat down with their friends
To laugh at such a disgrace.

Lauren Caroline Browne (10)
Newbuildings Primary School, Newbuildings

The Singing Goldfish

One morning on the edge of my bed,
I had the weirdest dream,
it was stuck in my head.
It was all about my goldfish friend
and his girlfriend, Trout.
As they sailed on the greatest boat built,
so grand even third class had fresh quilts!
But as it began to sink,
he began to think.
He sung his fish heart out.
So next time, you have a dream
Don't purchase Amazon Prime.

Rory Blaney (10)
St Brigid's Primary School, Cloughmills

Chameleon Man

One day in the woods,
There could be a chameleon,
And it had a tail which was blue,
It had a stinger,
It was yellow,
It went up close,
It got a grip,
It stung me twice,
Then I felt funny,
I got really dizzy,
I started to run,
But I fell asleep,
My trousers were green,
Most importantly, I could fly,
I had powers,
Thanks, chameleon!

Dara Waide (10)
St Brigid's Primary School, Cloughmills

My Sausage Aeroplane

My sausage aeroplane wasn't as good
As I planned,
A dog ate the bacon propellors,
The cloud monsters used my fudge tail wings
For breakfast,
A greedy man ate my pickle engines,
Without the engines,
We had to use our lettuce parachutes,
As the plane started to drop,
Everyone in Cloughmills and Dunloy
Had a free breakfast.

Jack Hardy McAuley (10)
St Brigid's Primary School, Cloughmills

My Guardian Angel!

My guardian angel is the best there'll be,
Because my guardian angel is the one they'll see,
For my guardian angel counts one, two, three,
And then my room is tidy,
And my hair is super straight,
My guardian angel is the one that'll be
Never forgotten and always remembered,
For she's the one they'll see!

Clare McNeilly (10)
St Brigid's Primary School, Cloughmills

My Crazy Dream

One night I woke up with a fright,
I turned on the light,
It was very bright
When I opened my eyes, I saw the guys
At Old Trafford in Manchester,
I was dabbing with Pogba,
High fiving with Lingard,
Taking free kicks with Rashford,
And saving shots with De Gea,
What a night in the 'Theatre of Dreams'!

Conor McCann

St Brigid's Primary School, Cloughmills

My Unsuccessful Parachuting In Space!

I went up, not down,
My parachute got burned
By the flames of a rocket,
I hopped from asteroid to asteroid,
I touched a star but that didn't go well,
An asteroid hit me,
I landed on the moon,
I felt numb,
My clothes floated off me,
I didn't make it to Earth,
And I was abducted by aliens!

Daniel Redmond (10)
St Brigid's Primary School, Cloughmills

What's Beyond The Universe?

Have you ever wondered
What's beyond the universe?
I have!
It might be a place that no one goes,
Or a place that no one knows,
Right round the corner,
Right through the door,
There could be a feast,
For all you know,
Although,
There could be something completely different!

Niamh Corr (11)
St Brigid's Primary School, Cloughmills

My Cookie Car

My cookie car didn't go as expected,
The chairs were all lumpy,
A dog ate my steering wheel,
The birds pecked on my ceiling,
The chocolate chips melted,
So I couldn't see out my window,
I crashed and it crumbled into dust,
But it tasted really yummy
When I ate it all up!

Erin Brennan (10)
St Brigid's Primary School, Cloughmills

Landing On Burger Planet

We are about to land on Burger Planet,
Five, four, three, two, one,
We are here, let's have some fun!
This can't be real, can it?
Food everywhere for everyone.

Which sides to have, coleslaw, salad or maybe
chips?
Top the burger with onions and sauce,
It looks so good, I'm licking my lips,
That was tasty, so tell your boss.

How's about something to wash it down?
Slush puppy, Fanta, water or Coke?
So many to choose from, I thought with a frown,
But if I get them all I think I will choke.

Time to indulge in something sweet,
Cakes, custard, Flakes and ice cream,
It's not that often I get such a treat,
Is this real or just a dream?

Eunan Beggs (10)
St Mary's Primary School, Pomeroy

Candy Planets

As I looked upon the sky,
I saw some bright colours that dazzled my eye,
Oh I wondered as to what it could be,
Is it a sweet treat just waiting for me?
Is it Mercury number one,
That is covered in chocolate buttons,
And next to the sun?
Or Venus, the hottest of them all?
Tastes just like a fireball.
Earth, of course, home to every boy and girl,
The green and blue colours of edible pearls,
And there's Mars, which is covered in jars
Of sticky toffee bars.
Alongside Jupiter, the largest of all,
This bright, large, aniseed ball.
Saturn surrounded with sherbet-filled rice paper,
This was a very busy little baker,
Uranus and Neptune, two of a kind,
Well, there was nothing that I could find,
The last main planet, Pluto the snug
Is the tastiest little brown humbug

Now as I wake from my sleep,
I realise, I had a great night's sleep.

Chloe Murphy (10)
St Mary's Primary School, Pomeroy

Going To Hogwarts

Harry and Ron Weasley in Gryffindor,
Draco, Crabbe and Goyle in Slytherin,
Cedric is Hufflepuff, Cho Chang's Ravenclaw,
All brought together for Harry's fave, Quidditch,
Annoy Harry at your peril,
"Expelliarmus" or "Stupefy" he'll cry,
Snape's lesson taught well
And now a potion unleashed to try,
Hagrid, McGonagall and Dumbledore keep an eye
on the house battle,
Hoping that no one gets turned into cattle,
They all came together at the end of the game,
A journey of learning to be had for the brave.

Daniel Cullen (10)
St Mary's Primary School, Pomeroy

The Elf That Lived In The Fridge!

There was once a silly elf in the fridge,
He laughed and sang all through the day
His friends would come and visit him,
And elf games they would play!
They swam in the juice jug,
They had a bath in the butter
While having a snowball fight with peas,
A jolly song they would mutter.
When morning comes and the sun comes out,
It's time for elves to get out of sight
They head off home to get some rest,
Ready for another night of mess!

Caitlin Mary Stewart (10)
St Mary's Primary School, Pomeroy

A Bobbly Goblin

Down, down, down,
I went through the darkness
And landed with a bump,
I saw a goblin with bubbles
Foaming out of his mouth,
The goblin shouted, "Follow! Follow me!"
So I followed the goblin to a magic door,
He led me to a wonderful place
Where goblins live,
It smelt like strawberry bubbles,
Trees floated on bubby clouds,
The tiny goblins bounced on fluffy craters,
A wonderful, magical world,
Could not be harmed.

Olivier Koprowski (10)
St Mary's Primary School, Pomeroy

The Giant's Challenge

One night I had a dream,
A giant did challenge me
To a magic handball game,
Far away in the fluffy clouds,
The game was about to start,
My nerves I couldn't control,
How would I ever return
The giant's mighty serve?
But I am Odhran the champion,
The greatest in all the Earth,
My returns outplayed the giant,
The magic clouds made the ball soar high,
Game ball!
I won,
But then I woke up in excitement.

Odhran Barrett (10)

St Mary's Primary School, Pomeroy

So Many Ideas

Today was very confusing,
I didn't know what to think about,
Pizza, school, work, family,
With lots of other ideas,
It was scary, cute, silly and delicious,
I didn't know what to think about,
I didn't know what day, time or year it was,
I heard people telling me what to do,
And I saw lots of things,
All I know, I am in a different world,
Oh, I just forgot,
I don't know what to do!

Clodagh Carey (10)
St Mary's Primary School, Pomeroy

My Magical Candy

My magical candy turned out to be money,
I wished all around me,
The pounds, dollars and euros
Blowing all around,
Making sounds,
Like the rustling of thunderstorms,
Swirling all around, what fun!

Cash rushing out of candy machines,
I would love if my dream came true,
I would live in a house full of cash,
And of course, my candy house too!

Kirsty Scott (10)

St Mary's Primary School, Pomeroy

Rainbows

Up, up very high,
There are clouds and rainbows in the sky,
Reds, blues, oranges and greens,
Lots of colours to be seen
Bands of colours fill the sky,
Jump, jump, jump up high,
But never ever touch the sky,
Rainbow, rainbow with frowns or smiles,
Looking for the crock of gold
At the end of the rainbow,
Where it touches the ground.

Darragh Rafferty (10)
St Mary's Primary School, Pomeroy

The Dragon Egg

Instead of a chick coming out of the egg,
A dragon appeared instead
That ended my excitement,
And that of my parents too
The little dragon was weird indeed,
A mess she created around the house,
She was good at putting the fire on,
I love my pet dragon, she is so nice,
She loves me too,
Forever to keep inside my warm house.

Caitlin Graham (10)
St Mary's Primary School, Pomeroy

Playing Football On The Clouds

Playing football on the clouds,
It's not as easy as it seems,
No bouncing ball,
Just floating ball,
Catching is extreme

Play football on the clouds,
It's not as easy as it seems,
The fluffy clouds,
Are huffy clouds,
Making my ball unseen.

Oliver Thomas Grimes (10)
St Mary's Primary School, Pomeroy

Underground World

A slippy, slidey slide,
A soft landing spot,
Ended up in a strange delicious spot,
From money growing on trees,
To houses made of chocolate
Strange little elves peeping round every corner,
Got up and realised it was true,
I had fallen into a magical world.

Aidan Devlin (9)
St Mary's Primary School, Pomeroy

Candyfloss Tree

I woke up one sunny morning
And went outside to play,
I saw something shiny,
All of a sudden, a huge tree came,
Speeding up with me on top,
I fell off with a bang,
The tree came over and lifted me up,
I sat there and the tree read me a book.

Ella-Mae Woods (9)

St Mary's Primary School, Pomeroy

Down At The Yard

Off to the yard, we do go,
Whether the weather is fine or snow,
Once there, we brush and shovel poo,
Until the stable is as good as new
Then onto Peter we do start,
To brush and comb till there's no mark,
Tail and mane brushed and plaited,
Legs all white and definitely not splatted
Bum all shiny as a new pin,
We can nearly see our faces in,
Now for the tack, hope it's clean,
'Cause if not, it would be mean
Out to the arena, we do go,
To put into practice what we know
Perhaps we will learn a thing or two,
That's if Peter doesn't lose a shoe
Back to the stable now to be snug and warm,
On his rug which is a little worn
Water, hay, carrot and a hug,
Then I go home to be warm and snug.

Dara Flynn (10)
St Patrick's Primary School, Mullanaskea

Inside Games

I was once inside a video game,
I didn't know what was going on
I noticed I was in a game,
I thought of all the fun I could have,
I met my favourite character,
He was really cool,
His name was Drift.

I moved on to the next game,
I turned into my character,
I played a few rounds at this game,
I decided to go to the disco,
I met the DJ,
I was so excited that I jumped off the ground,
It was very fun.

I started to dance in the disco,
He played my favourite disc,
There was a prize for the best dancer,
I started to try really hard,
I did the floss, twist, splits, dabs

All dances I could think of,
It tests if I'm good at dancing.

I won the competition,
I was back in the normal world,
I was very tired so I decided to go to bed,
Mummy said, "Where have you been?"
I said, "You won't believe!"
Mummy said, "Well, you must be tired,
Time to rest your head."

Jude Noel Patrick Trainor (9)

St Patrick's Primary School, Mullanaskea

A Tasty Solar System

After my rocket catapulted into orbit,
It began to feel quite calm
As I gazed out at the solar system,
I saw Saturn's rings were made of jam!
A meteor shower of Minstrels
Shot quietly through the night sky,
Just as I saw that the moon
Was a mass of cookie dough,
And Mercury was made of pie!
Mars oozed with caramel,
Jupiter was a ball of gum,
Crunchie stars glowing,
My tummy was going numb,
On and on my rocket went,
Past every tasty thing,
Until I got to the last planet,
To see a very boring thing,
Neptune was a maths book,
With sums all bursting out,
This was no laughing matter

"Help!" I began to shout,
I wished I could go back to my usual school day,
Then I heard the science teacher say,
"Hurry, class, it's time for dinner!"
At last!

Lorcan Doherty (9)

St Patrick's Primary School, Mullanaskea

The Mouse In The House

Away down the lane,
There was an old house,
A dark old house,
An empty frightening house.

In the old house,
Lived a lonely mouse,
Yet a playful mouse.

As I walked by one day,
It ran away,
He whispered, "Come in,
Come in and play?"
The mouse is talking,
Should I run away?

I opened the door and could not believe
The sight that greeted me,
There was a cat and a rat
And a bird with a hat,
And a bear lying down who looked very fat.

They asked me for supper,
Or even for a cuppa,
We sang some songs
And had such fun,
Soon it was time to leave my team,
But suddenly I woke up,
And it was all a dream.

Enya Moss (9)
St Patrick's Primary School, Mullanaskea

Jump As High As The Moon

How did she do it? You may as,
The cow I replied,
With a glint in my eye,
She bounced and bounced
'Til no one could see,
Up she went,
Like a huge, big bee,
Over she went on the crescent moon,
It was my turn,
Now how will I do?
My weapon of choice was an elastic band,
If I make it, I will be Superman!
I stretched the band as far as I could,
And followed the cow on her trip to the moon,
Higher and higher I went at full speed,
Fast approaching my destiny,
I heard no noise,
Not even a mouse,
Down below I saw my house

The moon I have launched,
In wonderful space,
Surrounded by stars,
What an amazing place!

Luke McCaffrey (10)

St Patrick's Primary School, Mullanaskea

The 1st Of December

On the first of December,
I will always remember,
Children playing,
Air swaying,
And a whole lot more.

When I woke up today,
On one of my favourite days,
I looked outside but it was dry,
I couldn't believe my eyes.

I couldn't believe the weather news lied,
I was so sad I even cried,
Then the phone call came,
Mum told me the news,
"School is on today,
The weather's exactly the same!"

On the first of December,
I will always remember,
What is in store

Weather news lying,
Me crying,
And a whole lot more.

Shaun Fitzpatrick (10)
St Patrick's Primary School, Mullanaskea

Find A Dragon

I was out for a walk,
I saw a cave,
I went into the cave
And I saw a big nest,
I looked into the nest,
I saw a strange thing,
It was a dragon,
It had large wings
And sharp teeth,
I felt brave
So I got on its back,
It liked me
And it didn't throw me off,
Most importantly,
It didn't want to eat me,
It flew out of the cave,
Up into the blue sky,
I could see small trees and houses
And people looked like ants,
Its stomach rumbled

So it dived down to a lake to feed,
And I jumped off
And ran away.
This was the best day ever.

Broccan Leonard (9)

St Patrick's Primary School, Mullanaskea

A Winter's Day

It was the first of December,
I could remember,
As I looked through my curtains,
I saw the snow,
There was tons of snow,
It lay outside my window,
Then I heard the pattering paws of the dog
In the mountains of snow,
Mum was making coffee,
I heard the kettle boiling,
I could smell the morning toast,
I grabbed my coat and hat,
Then ran outside,
Me and my friends threw snowballs
And made snowmen all day,
I came inside and sat by the fire,
Mum told me that it was time for bed,
My parents said, "Goodnight,"
And I went to sleep for the rest of the night.

Emily O'Connor (11)
St Patrick's Primary School, Mullanaskea

The Small Snow Leopard

I'm a snow leopard who lives in Nepal,
And I'm very small,
To be exact, two feet long,
But I am very strong.

My diet is yaks, ibex and sheep,
I love to eat them,
They taste so sweet.

I live in snowy conditions all day long,
The reason I eat my prey
Is to keep me healthy and very strong.

My coat is white and furry,
With black spots,
After all, they call me
The leopard with dots.

I don't know why I do not grow,
Maybe it is all the snow,
Wait! What is that long thing down below?
It's actually just my tail you know.

Leon Moore (8)
St Patrick's Primary School, Mullanaskea

Visiting Space

One year ago, or maybe two,
I had the idea to visit the moon,
So off I went,
I built my ship,
It really was quite the trip.
On my way round the stars,
I stumbled upon a planet called Mars,
I played on the planet til noon,
Until I wanted to go to the moon.
So off I went through the stars,
Just like I did on my way to Mars,
I played for the rest of the afternoon,
After I landed on the moon.
Mercury, Venus, Neptune too,
Are all the planets I hope to see soon,
But right here on Earth I'm happy to be,
Dreaming of space
And the places I'll see.

Isabella Wright (10)
St Patrick's Primary School, Mullanaskea

My Cookie Planet

I once had a cookie planet,
It was the best one in the chocolate Milky Way,
If I wanted a snack,
I did not have to pay,
I nibbled at the houses,
They were really nice,
My mum made nice cakes,
I sometimes took a slice,
I woke up one morning,
The sun was very bright,
When I went outside I had an awful fright,
It was not the milkshake ocean,
That was good as new,
It was the sun,
It was melting the chocolate,
The gummy people were sinking,
Sinking fast,
I tried to run to the phone,
But I could not move,
I realised that I was sinking too!

Michael McGowan (9)
St Patrick's Primary School, Mullanaskea

The Lion

I'm a lion, big and tall,
I'm the top predator of them all,
I am strong and tough,
And I play real rough.

I like to eat lots of meat
And stand really still on my feet,
In the sky, birds fly,
They want to play games but then they lie.

I'm from Africa,
And some other countries,
I use my paws to wipe out the fleas
Because they have a bad disease.

I catch my prey using my paws,
And take them down using my claws,
I take an antelope down,
And then take the zebra down,
And then all the animals give me a frown.

Adam Forster (9)
St Patrick's Primary School, Mullanaskea

The Ladybird Who Couldn't Fly

Sitting in the garden on a sunny summer's day,
When a ladybird came my way,
It had jet-black spots on a bright red back,
With tiny black legs,
Then it began to crawl on my hand,
I sat there watching to see when it would fly,
But it just kept crawling on my hand,
I noticed its wing,
It wasn't smooth like it should have been,
It was ruffled and wrinkled,
And I knew it couldn't fly,
So I felt a little sad,
As it crawled off my hand,
And disappeared into the long grass,
As the red and black turned into light green.

Grainne Gallagher (9)
St Patrick's Primary School, Mullanaskea

My Magic Burger

I have got a magic burger,
And it's sitting in front of me,
It's really big
And I'm going to eat it for tea.

It was made by fairies,
Using sparkle magic dust,
And eating the burger
Is a definite must.

Here goes one big bite,
And I'm as happy as can be,
I'm flying over the clouds, away to a party,
The party has elves, magicians and unicorns too,
We play hopscotch and peek-a-boo.

Now it's time to go home
And finish my tea,
Another bit of the burger
Is a definite for me.

Aisling Trainor (9)
St Patrick's Primary School, Mullanaskea

A Snowy Day

I lay in bed as long as I could,
I heard Mum talking about a day off,
Went and got my coat,
Put it on and put up my hood,
Away I went to build a snowman,
Letting off a cough,
I heard my brother coming out to play,
He actually came out with a tray,
We went up sledging in the field,
My dad went to ask for a tie,
He's not going to work, I don't know why,
We came inside all cold and wet,
Hot chocolate is what I went to get,
I went and turned on the heat,
Then I sat down on a seat,
Snuggled up and watched a movie.

Michael Cleary (11)
St Patrick's Primary School, Mullanaskea

Riding A Lightning Bolt

All of a sudden I was on a lightning bolt,
It was blurry and wet,
I could barely see where I was going,
I could just about make out
that I was zooming over Ireland.
As I was zooming in the sky,
there was another planet, made of chocolate.
I put my hand out and grabbed the chocolate,
as much as I could!
And, as soon as I was about to eat it,
I crashed into Ireland with a thud.
I fell back and landed on my doorstep,
I sat down and found chocolate
all around me on the ground,
This was the best adventure ever!

Tomás McGirr (9)
St Patrick's Primary School, Mullanaskea

The Flying Drum Kit

I was about to play my drum kit,
But it shot into the sky,
I could barely see it,
As it was very high!

I tried a thirty-foot ladder,
But it was just too short,
I felt like I was in so much trouble,
I thought I'd end up in court!

I was so worried I called 999,
The rescue team came,
But oh dear, it was just too high!

Then I had a brilliant idea,
I used a piece of rope,
Spinning and spinning, away it goes,
Then my drum kit came back,
Just like I hoped.

Oisín Murphy (9)
St Patrick's Primary School, Mullanaskea

Birthday Fail

I remember the day where this story takes place,
It was my fifth birthday and we were all in haste,
But we looked outside,
It had snowed so we all went to hide.

Mum panicked, Dad became arty,
Granny had the idea to call off my party,
I screamed because my brother threw a snowball
at me,
Then I ran outside in glee.

In the end, Mum called off my party,
Someone still gave me a present,
His name was Marty,
We had my party another day,
But yet, I still did not get my own way.

Ellie-Mae Clarkson (11)
St Patrick's Primary School, Mullanaskea

My Dreams

I fall asleep on a cloud,
When I make myself proud,
I seep through black holes,
And bump into poles.

I'm a brave superhero,
Rollerskating on Pluto.

I'm an actor on TV,
As I sit on my settee,
And there I am,
Making a plan, to conquer the land!

I'm a princess in purple,
With a crown of yellow,
Hoping to marry that handsome fellow.

As I snuggle up tight,
To my teddy at night,
I wait for my dreams,
To take another flight.

Sophie Mae McGrory (10)
St Patrick's Primary School, Mullanaskea

A Ride On A Unicorn In Space

Zoom!

What was that?
Oh, that was me,
Full of glee,
On a unicorn's back,
Full of attack.

We soared through the sky,
And watched the stars go by,
We flew through Mars,
We saw no cars.

We zoomed around Saturn,
And made a pattern,
We flew around Venus,
I felt like a genius.

To the moon, we landed,
Single-handed

And finally back home,
Through the ozone.

What a wonderful dream,
That made me beam.

Charley Gilmurray (10)
St Patrick's Primary School, Mullanaskea

Hooray

I lie in bed filled with dread
Of the morning ahead,
School!
I get nervous,
I look outside, I see the snow,
Lying like doughnut dough,
I hear my mum asking people
To mind me today,
And I say hooray,
My childminder comes,
I say, "We're off today!"
But then my mum's phone goes off
And she says to the childminder,
"We don't need you today!"
I feel like I'm about to cry,
I say goodbye to my childminder,
And I go to school.

Daniel Harvey (11)
St Patrick's Primary School, Mullanaskea

Easter Wonderland

Easter is that time of year,
It fills everyone's hearts with cheer,
Lambs are born, little chicks too,
And the Easter bunny makes deliveries to you.

Chocolate eggs and sweets galore,
A little more than the year before,
Flowers in bloom, birds singing clearly,
All the more reason we love it so dearly.

Easter egg hunts and sun-filled hours,
Will treats be sweet or will they be sour?
Bunting, decorations and colour so grand,
All adds to my Easter Wonderland.

Rian John McSorley (9)
St Patrick's Primary School, Mullanaskea

The Slowest Cheetah

There once was a cheetah from Tempo,
Whose speed was not right, he was slow,
As hard as he pushed, as hard as he tried,
He was left in the dust and he cried and cried.

"I'm a cheetah, not a fajita,
I'm meant to be fast,
But why oh why am I always last?"

One day, feeling low,
He saw a Lamborghini in tow
And a lightbulb went on in his head,
"If I can't be speedy,
I'll just be greedy,
And buy a red sports car instead."

Patrick Toal (9)
St Patrick's Primary School, Mullanaskea

Spooky Dream

Spooky night, spooky night,
If you stay up too late,
You'll get an awful fright,
During the night,
I witnessed a dreadful,
Funny, wacky thing,
I saw zombies riding bikes,
And the boogie man
Picking his nose,
Skeletons doing Fortnite dances,
And worst of all,
My nan in her granny pants,
Ants eating onions
And not to mention,
I hadn't played Fortnite in hours,
But then I woke up to my mummy shouting,
"Get up for school!"

Makayla Lealan (10)
St Patrick's Primary School, Mullanaskea

Dream Come True

As I travel down the highway in my Scania 143,
I cannot believe what I can see,
The highway stretching in front of me,
It's such a sight to see,
As I grind through the gears,
I show no fear,
As I pulled into the truck stop,
I got a sausage and egg bap,
I've got a long way to go,
But I'll go with the flow,
After my forty-five, I sure feel alive,
Horns honking, engines roaring,
It's clearly not boring,
This is my dream come true.

Kilian Trainor (8)
St Patrick's Primary School, Mullanaskea

The Dream

Oh no!
I just woke up this morning to find...

My tractor is flying,
My cows are talking,
My bales are dancing,
My digger is walking.

My shed is flashing,
My trailer is swinging,
My tanker is slurping,
My wellies are singing.

My spade is conducting,
My fields are pulling faces,
My trees are flossing,
My wheelbarrows are having races.

Oh yes!
I just woke up this morning to find...
It was only a dream!

Cormac Cox (8)

St Patrick's Primary School, Mullanaskea

Snow Day

I love winter,
When you cosy up to Nan,
And then you go outside
And build a snowman.

I know, I know,
It all sounds so crazy,
But to sit around the fire
With a cup of hot choc and be really lazy.

A day without tests,
Homework or maths,
But still with friends
And having a good laugh.

And to play outside,
With your dog in the snow,
When they try to eat it,
You need to shout, "No!"

Aoibhín Campbell (9)
St Patrick's Primary School, Mullanaskea

The Big Game

All to play for in the county final,
Lisbellaw 2-16,
Erne Gaels 2-16.

It was the final two minutes remaining,
Young McCann just put another point over,
But Erne Gaels put another point over as well.

With fifty seconds left,
Cleary takes a puck,
Erne Gaels takes him out of it,
The sliotar hit the crossbar,
But McCann ran up to the square,
And slashes the sliotar
In the back of the net,
What a win!

Ryan McCann (11)
St Patrick's Primary School, Mullanaskea

A Prince And Princess

I once had a dream about a fairy princess,
She went to a party in a magical, sparkly dress,
She glided through the door
With a wand in her hand,
She danced to the music
That was played by the band,
She met a handsome prince,
Who was lovely and sweet,
He asked the princess to dance,
What a lovely treat,
He asked her to be his wife,
The princess said yes,
They married the next day
And had a wonderful life.

Hannah Hobbs (8)
St Patrick's Primary School, Mullanaskea

My Underwater House

I wish I could live under the sea,
Imagine how fun it would be,
I could swim around all day long,
And hear a mermaid sing a song,
I could play with the dolphin and fish,
It would be brilliant, oh how I wish
I could take the submarine to school,
Oh, it really would be so cool,
The only thing I would worry about,
Would be turning blue,
But someday I hope my dream will come true.

Hannah Lynch (9)

St Patrick's Primary School, Mullanaskea

The Dreaded Clothes

When I went to bed
On that winter's night,
I was filled with joy and a lot of delight,
The reason for this was because school was closed,
And I knew I wouldn't have to wear
The dreaded clothes,
I started to fill with fear,
But hoped what I thought wouldn't be true,
To my relief, school was still closed,
I was glad I didn't have to put on
The dreaded clothes.

Cathy Britton (10)
St Patrick's Primary School, Mullanaskea

Would You Enjoy A Day In Sugar Land?

I loved my day in Sugar Land,
With snowmen made of fluffy marshmallows,
Wearing a strawberry lace scarf,
Looking so smart with his Smartie eyes,
A gingerbread house set on green icing grass,
I may have eaten a bit,
Chunky, chocolate trees,
A runny, caramel lake and a gummy sun,
Floating everywhere,
My day in Sugar Land was sugartastic,
Would you enjoy a day in Sugar Land?

Ellen Cleary (9)

St Patrick's Primary School, Mullanaskea

I'm Going On Holiday

I'm going on my holiday,
My passport and ticket in my hand,
Up, up the steps I go,
Onto the plane to fly away,
I sit on my seat and fasten my belt,
The engines rumble underneath me,
Faster, faster, I'm forced back into my seat,
We are taking off,
Up, up high we shoot into the sky,
I look out my window,
Watching the clouds go by,
I'm going on my holiday.

Robert Balfour (9)
St Patrick's Primary School, Mullanaskea

Otter

I am an otter who lives in the sea,
It is very icy,
So please help me.

I can do twirls and twists,
I can do anything
As long as it's on my list.

I am all on my own now,
Since Mum and Dad passed away.
Oil spills and pollution was how.
I'm fine on my own now,
But when it comes to the night,
I get an awful fright.

Don't pollute.

Charlie Keegan (9)
St Patrick's Primary School, Mullanaskea

A Winter Day

When I woke up,
I saw the snow,
It really did glow,
It was piled like a tower,
It felt like powder,
I grabbed my coat,
And ran like a goat,
I went to the park
But it was getting dark,
I went home,
And played on my phone,
I heard the tapping of the snow
Against my bedroom window,
It was really tempting to go and play,
I was really enjoying my day.

Bella Maye Abraham (11)
St Patrick's Primary School, Mullanaskea

My Pet Is A Genie

I have a genie that is my pet,
And into a mermaid she did turn me,
It was so amazing,
My hair was turquoise slime
That sparkled blue,
My skin was all colours of the rainbow too.

And my tail was pearlescent
That changed colour in the light,
That gave the sharks such a fright,
But brought dolphins over to me,
Who gave me a sloppy kiss
On the right.

Carágh Mary-Kate Sliman (9)
St Patrick's Primary School, Mullanaskea

The Sweet Stuff

Why oh why is sugar so yummy?
When Mum says it's not good for my tummy,
Sweets, chocolate, buns and cakes,
Apple pie and strawberry shakes,
This is what I want to eat,
But they have to be a treat,
Then again, on thinking twice,
Cavities and diabetes do not sound nice,
So I'd better listen to what they say,
And keep the sweet stuff until treat day!

Alex Beacom (7)
St Patrick's Primary School, Mullanaskea

I Love Snow

I love the way it sparkles and crunches,
I don't like that you get so cold,
When I look out the window,
The fields look bleach white,
When I go sledging my legs are so wet,
When you put your hands in the snow,
It feels soft,
Sometimes the snow on the trees looks fluffy,
Sometimes when I imagine,
I imagine that it is marshmallow,
I love snow.

Sorcha Leonard (8)
St Patrick's Primary School, Mullanaskea

When My Snowman Falls

I'm a little snowman,
Short and fat,
I have my scarf
And I have my hat,
When the sun comes out,
I cannot play,
Then I slowly just melt away,
My owners are really sad
And sometimes get really mad,
The snow melts and goes away,
Then the children get sad
And I wish I could stay,
I wish I could stay with the children
Another day.

Russell Mikiewicz Lumayad (8)
St Patrick's Primary School, Mullanaskea

Curly Shampoo

Dad bought shampoo for curly hair,
He brought it home without a care,
We used it and *wow*,
We have Michael Jackson hair,
It makes me feel dizzy,
My big hair,
Nothing can tame it,
It's as big as a chair,
You guessed it, it's my hair,
But I don't care if people stare,
Because I am special
And my hair belongs to me.

Oran Fitzpatrick (10)
St Patrick's Primary School, Mullanaskea

Through The Air

I was waiting for two o'clock,
I waited and waited,
Then I saw this thing in the air,
It swooped down at my doorway
And then I walked outside
And hopped on its back,
It was magical, fearsome, gigantic
And breathed fire,
We swooped up to the sky,
I said this is amazing,
More fun than the party,
Then I screamed in joy.

Daithí Shannon (10)

St Patrick's Primary School, Mullanaskea

Cakes On A Cloud

Oh, how I love cake,
But not really on the ground,
I make my cakes up in the clouds,
Vanilla, chocolate, strawberry or lemon,
These are my favourite kinds,
Light and fluffy are the clouds,
Are my cakes made from clouds,
Good question, so they are,
Because my cloud is made from...
Candyfloss!

Niamh Murphy (10)
St Patrick's Primary School, Mullanaskea

Under The Cherry Blossom Tree

Under the cherry blossom tree,
There is so much I can see,
As I gaze upon the big blue sky,
I can see the birds flying by,
The sweet smell of flowers fills the air,
Nature's gift I wish I could share,
I can't wait to see what this summer brings,
I tell myself I won't miss a thing.

Ellie-Mae Murphy (11)
St Patrick's Primary School, Mullanaskea

Have A Dragon As A Pet

To have a dragon as a pet,
Probably really hard, I bet,
You have to give it lots of food,
To keep it in a happy mood,
Give it water and let it drink,
But don't let it swim because it would sink,
Dragons are really hard to keep,
Because they always snore when they're asleep.

Cohen Murphy (10)
St Patrick's Primary School, Mullanaskea

Spring And Summer

Flowers are closed and lambs are sleeping,
Stars are up, the moon is peeping,
While the birds are silence-keeping,
Sleep, my baby, fall a-sleeping,
Donkey riding, donkey riding,
Hey ho and away we go,
Where the folk all shout hooray,
Let's hope the bees don't swarm.

Tara Annie Mcmanus (8)
St Patrick's Primary School, Mullanaskea

My Pet Elephant

My pet elephant,
She has two wings,
She flies me to school,
And she even sings,
Mum and Dad said they can't see her,
And even said she isn't real,
But I know she is,
Because she always peels my bananas,
When I'm older, she'll still be my pet elephant.

Eva-Alexandra Nelson (10)
St Patrick's Primary School, Mullanaskea

Sunbathe On A Cloud

I woke on a cloud,
Flying high,
Like a fluffy marshmallow in the sky,
The sun was hot,
the sky was blue,
I looked down,
Oh, what a view,
A bird flew past,
Oh, so fast,
I lay back and closed my eyes,
And the sun shone on me.

Tara McCusker (9)
St Patrick's Primary School, Mullanaskea

Winter

While it was severely snowing,
I heard a terrifying rumbling sound from above,
It was a while before I figured out what it was,
Ever heard an avalanche?
It was a bit like that,
Really though,
It was just snow falling off the roof of the flat.

Eoghan Campbell (10)
St Patrick's Primary School, Mullanaskea

I Love To Dance

Every day I like to dance,
I got new shoes,
To help me prance.

My dancing shoes are pretty cool,
They help me jump and point my toes,
It keeps me fit to dance loads.

When I go to feis,
I feel happy,
In my new dress.

Erun Farry (9)
St Patrick's Primary School, Mullanaskea

No More Elephants

One morning I went to the zoo,
I didn't know what to do,
So I went to look at the elephants,
There was only one thing wrong,
They were all gone,
Later that day, we found them
Singing a song.

Reuben Nathan Abraham (8)
St Patrick's Primary School, Mullanaskea

No More Tart For Bart

There once was a small boy called Bart,
Who ate too much ice cream and tart,
He ran to his mummy,
With pains in his tummy,
And vowed never to eat it again.

Nathan Hanna (9)
St Patrick's Primary School, Mullanaskea

Night

Night is a crook, a criminal, a thief,
Trees sway silently in the breeze,
Night spreads swiftly along the sky,
Shadows wander silently around the street,
Night is as sly as a fox,
Creeping around, watching children sleep,
Yet he does not make a sound.

But wait!
The sun's rays slowly seep through
The black blanket,
Skies turn bright blue as the sun emerges,
Suddenly the Earth is full with colour once again,
Her radiant smile makes the breeze soft and warm,
The trees stand tall and straight like a soldier,
Butterflies flap their delicate wings
And the ice cream man's rhyme plays
Around the small streets,
She wakes our wonderful world
Like a guardian angel.

Freya Whitten (11)
Sunnylands Primary School, Carrickfergus

Night

Night is a crook with no mercy,
He snatches away all the light of the day,
Leaving us with darkness,
All hope is lost as soon as the sun
Scampers away,
Hiding from the criminal,
Night replaces clouds with stars,
And the sun with a moon that shines dimly,
He makes it quiet enough so that we can sleep,
But he only does this to make sure
He has no witnesses!
As he creeps around, we snore softly,
Not knowing what this horrible creature is up to,
Who knows when he'll strike again?

But wait!
The sun's glowing rays pierce through
The dark night sky,
Slowly at first,
But then exploding through gracefully,
As she wakes us up,
She peers through our windows

To show, once again, the sun has conquered
The villain called 'Night',
While we get up to stretch our legs,
We say, "Good morning Sun!"
We are very grateful that she protects us,
Then she surprises us with towns,
Hills and glistening lakes,
That were once consumed with darkness
And are now splendid and alive!
She winks at us,
Unable to hide her excitement
As the day begins.

Ellie McCrory (10)
Sunnylands Primary School, Carrickfergus

Night

Night steals the light from our house
Every time we close the curtains,
He leaves us without our light,
While he moves shadily across the world,
Making sure he captures the day
Without giving it a chance to fight back,
Everything hesitates when night falls,
Trying to hide but can't run away too far,
Leaving us thinking,
Is the night a demon in disguise?
While the stars fearfully twinkle
In the night sky.

But always after night,
The sun comes out for a while,
Beaming hot,
Bringing life to the world,
It glows magically taking away the dark night,
Making everyone happy,
Opens the curtains,
Everybody smiles with joy

Happy night has gone,
The sun is bringing happiness
To everybody's day and encouraging people,
Children out having a great time playing,
Eating ice cream,
Having a barbecue and water fights,
Going to the beach, playing ball games,
Swimming in the ocean,
Day will always beat night.

Madison McClean (10)

Sunnylands Primary School, Carrickfergus

Night

The night comes,
Everybody's scared,
The houses turn off,
Closing their doors like a mouth,
The sun says, "It's time for me to go!"
The night takes complete control over the world,
Stealing the day,
Day says, "Help!"
But night has no mercy,
Night stamps on day now,
No daylight, no life,
All dark,
Moon says, "Ha ha, you lose!"
Stars look reluctant,
They didn't want to look,
The stars flinched every time
The sun got stamped on.

But the sun emerges from the
Bottom of the sea,
Night says, "Oh I think I have to leave now,"

Sun takes control,
Bringing life, light, colour and more,
The brightness of the sun,
Explodes the moon into smithereens.

Katie-Leigh Moore (10)
Sunnylands Primary School, Carrickfergus

Night

When the night creeps swiftly in,
To come and steal the light,
He puts on a display
Of all twinkling jewels he's stolen,
This sly criminal brings out the jewel
That he's most proud of,
Something we call the moon,
When he brings his darkness,
He brings his animals too,
He brings his bats and owls
To stalk the land,
When morning comes, he slides away,
Waiting for his time to come again.

But then! The glorious sun emerges
From behind the clouds,
Returning the light
That the nasty night stole,
Coming to wake the world up,
Bringing happiness that night has passed
And day has come again,
Making wonderful creatures emerge

From their homes
To praise the sunlight,
Day has conquered night!

Katie Hill (11)

Sunnylands Primary School, Carrickfergus

Night

Night slithers into my bedroom,
Capturing the sun in front of me,
The night forcing the stars to twinkle timidly,
As people watch from below,
As the stars stare from above,
The nifty night has won the war,
But out of the depths,
The stars timidly move away,
And the sun appears in front of the night,
But look!
It is a war,
The bubbling beams of day,
Versus the dark cloak of night,
The beams chipping away, getting stronger,
Wait! Everything changes as a flower appears,
Then the hill, then the silky green grass,
And the blue sky appears,
The beaming hot sun
Has done his work now,
We can hear the laughter of the children,
Playing water fights

And eating ice-cold ice cream,
All is back to normal for now!

Josh Hildrew (11)
Sunnylands Primary School, Carrickfergus

Night

Night is a slow, calm person,
Suddenly he turns and the night
Is a bad, cold feeling
That nobody likes now,
He had been stealing the light and sun,
There was no sun for two whole days now,
But then, all of a sudden,
Sun fought against night,
And night was to be put behind bars,
Until another calm night,
But will it be calm next time?

The sun will always win
Because loads of people love and cherish
The sun.

Dark takes away the light,
And the sun,
Just like a criminal,
The dark can be nice,
Or terrifying.

The sun goes to sleep at night time,
And the night goes to bed
When the sun comes out.

Jak Matthews (11)
Sunnylands Primary School, Carrickfergus

Unicorn Land

This crazy land
Has neon sand,
It has mermaid scales fresh from their tails,
We are turning into unicorns,
We are getting rainbow horns!
This is unicorn land,
It's very grand!
My sister is messing around,
She fell to the ground,
Now we are going to be banned
From this beautiful land!
I will miss you, cotton candy cloud,
The crowd was very loud,
DJ Rainbow's rock and roll music
had a big sound,
He should be crowned,
My friend Sweetie the unicorn
Has a fuzzy horn,
She loves popcorn,
I ate a bit of chocolate,
It was a big hit!

Amelia Dougherty (8)
Sunnylands Primary School, Carrickfergus

Night

The darkness of night,
Swiftly peeks through the window,
Sneaking along the hall
Till it gets to the living room,
The night creeps through the door,
And scarcely makes a sound,
Night settles down in the sky,
Amongst tiny, twirling stars
At exactly the same time.

But wait!
The sun's shining, mystical rays
Make their way through the deep, dark sky,
They shimmer like diamonds outside
On a sunny day,
They are like golden glitter,
Being lightly sprinkled
Onto dark, grey concrete,
That has been trampled on a thousand times.

Erynne-Leigh McKeown (11)
Sunnylands Primary School, Carrickfergus

Night

The night sneaks into my house,
Then into my bedroom,
At least it didn't take my pocket money!
But it has stolen the lovely daylight
Out of the house,
Everything is dark,
Then there is the shining light
And it is stars blinding me,
And then it was the moon!

But then the sun rose up
And fought to be back on its spot,
Then the sun was losing,
Because it wasn't morning still,
But when it was,
It won the fight,
And then there was colour, life,
Things all around us,
We were a happy family
And there was a rainbow.

Ellie Brown (10)
Sunnylands Primary School, Carrickfergus

Simon The Cat!

Simon the cat,
Took his Monday nap,
On his tender old blanket,
He woke up,
And stretched his back,
With a really big crack,
He looked outside with a big fright,
As a dog jumped up,
The less he spoke,
The more he heard the dog,
He peeked outside at the right time,
Because the dog wasn't there,
Simon went into the kitchen,
To get his blue ball,
And rumbled around with it,
It went under the couch,
Simon went under,
He also got stuck,
His bottom got stuck,
And his owner came down
And pulled him out!

Jade Graham (9)
Sunnylands Primary School, Carrickfergus

The Dino Fight

In the valley on a sunny day,
The dinos are here to stay.

It's before the Game Boy,
It's BC and the dinos have no toys.

Some are chomping on fern trees,
While others are snacking on meat.

A huge megalodon lurking in the deep, blue ocean,
Everything is calm while still in motion.

A big T-rex is very enormous,
But the diplodocus is amazingly humungous.

The dinos screamed, roared and struggled,
Because the meteor gave them trouble!

Yazmin Watson (9)
Sunnylands Primary School, Carrickfergus

Penguins On Ice

Welcome to our penguin's show,
It's crazy with all these penguins
Standing in a row,
There are Hop and Plop and Flippy Flop,
Showing their skills,
And not one is having a strop,
Skating here and skating there,
They are having fun everywhere,
Hop and Plop skate and try their best,
Flippy Flop is just better than all the rest,
Penguin TV will be in for a treat,
Watching all these dancing feet,
Enjoy the show,
And be careful when dancing in the snow.

Paige Holmes (9)

Sunnylands Primary School, Carrickfergus

Night Vs The Sun

Night crept into my room
And stole the sun before my eyes,
He was like a sly fox,
Waiting to pounce at anything!
He was clad in black, for people not to see him,
The next night he would strike again.

But look!
The sun has been discovered!
The cloak of the night has been banished,
The sun's smile is glowing,
The sun conquers the night,
Sun and night are like the police and a robber,
The sun will strike again.

Heidimarie Shaznay Hoey (11)
Sunnylands Primary School, Carrickfergus

Upside-Down Crazy Land

In Upside-Down Crazy Land,
Things are weird, things are grand
Money grows on silver trees,
Many houses are made of cheese.

In Upside-Down Crazy Land,
There is sparkling rainbow sand
A candy sun shines bright,
And the cupcake trampolines are quite a sight.

In Upside-Down Crazy Land,
You will see the watermelon band
When you see colourful posters,
You know it's time for rainbow roller coasters.

Anamika Ullas Nair (9)

Sunnylands Primary School, Carrickfergus

Crazy Creatures

Crazy creatures live everywhere,
They even live in the air,
Unicorns sit on clouds
And fairies fly around,
Dragons live in caves,
They sometimes like to have a rave,
They sometimes like to run free,
Even though it's time for tea!
In Candyland, it's such a sight,
They sometimes like to have funny fights,
It's the kind of fight
Where they dance and sing,
It really is the most crazy thing!

Jorja Beck (8)
Sunnylands Primary School, Carrickfergus

Life As A Unicorn

There was a unicorn that liked to prance,
She also liked to sing and dance,
Her name was Jorja,
She really liked food,
Even though she was rude,
Yesterday at school,
She went to the pool,
It really is against the rule!
She jumped off the diving board,
She yelled and squealed,
"This is so cool!"

Jessica Ross (9)
Sunnylands Primary School, Carrickfergus

Troll Land

The land was wet,
The bridge was broken,
I heard a sound,
It was all around,
The sound came from a cottage,
I went over,
The door was closed over,
I opened the door,
I went upstairs and saw a troll,
The roll was blue,
He had a lot of glue,
And he had the flu,
That's what the noise was!

Demi Sharkey (9)
Sunnylands Primary School, Carrickfergus

Blaze

He stands alone, handsome on his throne,
His eyes are shining like stars at night,
Oh, how I love my doggy knight,
He is brave and true,
His collar is a beautiful shade of blue,
Blaze stands in all his glory,
Each day with him tells a different story,
Treat your pet right,
For they are your friends at night.

Ollie McClean (9)
Sunnylands Primary School, Carrickfergus

The Fun Land

I came to a land and it was very fun,
It had pink sand and tan palm trees,
As I walked around,
There was a crowd,
They were very loud,
I walked home with my new friend,
His name was Ted,
I finally got home and was very tired,
It was really fun but I went to bed
To eat my bun.

Kendra Allen (8)
Sunnylands Primary School, Carrickfergus

The Squirrel

The squirrel hides in the trees all day,
He plays all day without any pay,
He jumps from branch to branch,
Out for some lunch,
His shiny coat gleams
In the sky,
As he dances up high and high,
I wish I had a squirrel's life,
Perhaps I would even get a lovely wife.

Harry Speirs (9)

Sunnylands Primary School, Carrickfergus

A Dragon Tale

There was a dragon called Bob,
He really likes corn on the cob,
Bob likes to play,
He also makes stuff out of clay,
Bob also makes stuff out of blocks
And rocks,
Bob loves bouncy things
And trees,
And loves eating delicious bees and cheese.

Kenzie Elliott (8)
Sunnylands Primary School, Carrickfergus

YOUNG WRITERS
INFORMATION

We hope you have enjoyed reading this book – and that you will continue to in the coming years.

If you're a young writer who enjoys reading and creative writing, or the parent of an enthusiastic poet or story writer, do visit our website **www.youngwriters.co.uk**. Here you will find free competitions, workshops and games, as well as recommended reads, a poetry glossary and our blog. There's lots to keep budding writers motivated to write!

If you would like to order further copies of this book, or any of our other titles, then please give us a call or visit **www.youngwriters.co.uk**.

Young Writers
Remus House
Coltsfoot Drive
Peterborough
PE2 9BF
(01733) 890066
info@youngwriters.co.uk

Join in the conversation!
Tips, news, giveaways and much more!

 YoungWritersUK    @YoungWritersCW